Persuasion

the Art of Influence and Convincing Others

Persuasion is Not Evil, It's just a Tool.
The Covert Language to Succeed in
Life, Love and Work

Written By

Abraham Goleman

Table of Contents

INTRODUCTION

Thank you for purchasing this book!

The idea behind being a persuasive person, which is the main objective of persuasion, is to get something in return. There is no sense in practicing the art of persuasion if there is nothing desired in return. Persuasion means to cause someone to do something specific. Therefore, some sort of gain is desired, some sort of result.

Enjoy your reading!

What Is Persuasion?

Persuasion is something that we experience daily. We are going to be persuaded by friends and family to help out on occasion. We will see many advertisements from companies that want to persuade us to purchase their products and not from competitors. We see persuasion so often that it is sometimes hard to realize that it could be bad and that a manipulator could try to use this against us.

How does one get people to think and behave differently and to follow their path? There will be many subtle ways to press your agenda without turning everyone off and making it seem like you have some sinister plan in the making. When it comes to persuasion, Robert Cialdini is well respected for some of his ideas on persuasion and how to do it successfully, whether your intentions are good or not.

According to Cialdini, six principles can be used to help out with the ideas of persuasion, and these six principles are going to include:

- Reciprocity: This is where you will do a small favor for someone, and then right away ask them to do one back.

- Commitment and consistency: This one holds the target of doing something because they have done it in the past.

- Social proof: This is when you convince the target to do something because it is popular, and everyone is doing it.

- Authority: Your target is more likely to do something if they believe you are an authority on that topic.

- Likeability: If you can become likable and see you as a friend, they are more likely to do what you ask.

- Scarcity: This is the fear that an item will be in short supply, so they want to get it.

Understanding Persuasion

and Its Significance

The main aim of every negotiation is to agree on an issue. In coming to that agreement, a major skill you need is persuasion. You should be able to persuade and convince the other party to agree with you.

Being good at persuasion is a vital part of a successful negotiation. It is a very important skill that you and everyone intend to have fruitful negotiations or intend to influence others. Persuasion is effectively marketing and selling your point of view to the other party. You have to persuade the other party to understand your viewpoint and even to accept it.

As an entrepreneur or an individual going into a negotiation, you should convince others to accept your ideas or your stance. For example, it is persuasion that would help you get your employer to increase your salary when you are negotiating a salary raise, and this would only happen if you can convince your employer about how valuable you have been and how a salary raise for you would be beneficial to both you and the company.

Persuasion is mostly giving people reasons why they should do something to be convinced to do it.

Contrary to what people believe about persuasion being a talent, it is a skill that can be learned and can be honed through practice. If you are still in doubt about why persuasion is important in negotiation and why you need to learn how to persuade people, here are some reasons.

Changing Mindsets

This appears to be the most apparent benefit of persuasion; however, it needs to be reiterated because of its importance.

When people come to the negotiation table, they come with their beliefs, mindsets, and attitudes. Sometimes, these beliefs or mindsets do not favor you, which means you have to change them through persuasion.

The mindsets or beliefs do not even have to be about the negotiation or the issue at hand. Sometimes they are about you, and you can use persuasion to change how the other party views you.

For example, a former negotiation with an earlier client earned you a bad reputation in the industry, the status of a wise businessperson who everyone should be wary of when transacting business. Now, when people have to do business with you, they are so careful, and they are always on the defense so much that the negotiation process rarely goes smoothly. With persuasion, you can convince the client that the reputation is false. You can influence them to stop being on the defense, and you will have a smooth negotiation process and get the best possible outcome.

Dispute Management

Paul is in a negotiation between the IT company he works at and a prospective client. A tactless colleague at the meeting has just said something the prospective client finds annoying. Tempers are flaring; words are being exchanged.

Paul decides to step in and do something. He is known as a tension diffuser at the office who can influence people to do his bidding. He calmly speaks to the client and then to his colleague. Apologies are exchanged, and everyone goes back to doing what they were doing earlier.

When you can persuade people as a skill, you will be able to deal with any disputes while negotiating. Sometimes, deals do not go through because they are open or latent disputes or rising tensions, and the two parties have gotten to a point where their emotions cloud their judgment. It takes persuasion skill to handle this and ensure that everyone goes back to the negotiation table and makes the deal.

This benefit of persuasion is particularly important because you should build relationships that leave room for further negotiation and business transactions after the initial negotiation.

Greater Sales

Stella is a businesswoman looking to sell her products. However, she is experiencing a drought when it comes to getting customers to buy the products she is selling. Also, there is the problem of competitors who have established brands in the industry getting most of the patronage. Stella wants customers to patronize her business. She wants customers to buy her products. Not only is Stella looking for new customers who have not purchased a similar product, but she is also hoping to get some of her competitors' customers. She needs to convince these customers to buy her products.

When you are promoting your product or service to a customer, your ability to persuade them to see why they should patronize is vital to making any successful sale. You need to convince your target market that you understand their needs and know how to provide great solutions to those needs.

Persuasion during sales will help you show the customer the merits of giving you their money. Persuasion is important for negotiating even the customer's price; if you want to make a sales deal happen, learn how to be persuasive.

Career Advancement

Everyone wants to grow. Whether it is transitioning to a new job or getting a promotion and a corresponding pay raise, career advancement is always welcome.

Career advancement also involves some negotiation. From negotiating your salary to negotiating with the firm's management you work for a promotion and a pay raise; you need to have good negotiation skills to get your desired outcome.

When it comes to getting your desired outcome in advancing your career, persuasion plays a significant role. Suppose you are applying for a new job. In that case, you should persuade your prospective employer to increase the initial offer that was made and pay you either the amount you are asking for or something close to that which would still be favorable to you. If you already work at a firm and you would like to take on more responsibility, you would like to be promoted, or you want a pay raise, you need to convince the firm's management to get the desired outcome.

One good thing about persuasion is that its effects are not limited to a single person. You can use it for large audiences. Suppose you are trying to pitch a product or service to a room full of potential investors beyond persuading one person to invest in the product. In that case, you can persuade all the potential investors to make your great offers.

After discovering how persuasion can be beneficial to you, you should learn the types of persuasion. Learning the types of persuasion is a step in the right direction for learning how to wield persuasion as a valuable skill while negotiating.

How to Become Persuasive?

How is it that some people are so good at convincing others to do things? How do some people manage to persuade others into things they wouldn't normally do? The skills of a manipulator and situation a person determines the extent to which one can be influenced. How much can a person persuade you is determined by your current state? For instance, if you are lonely, hungry, tired, or even needy somehow, then the chances of you being persuaded rise. Simply put, you can get a hungry man to do anything so long as you promise him a plate of food.

So, ensuring that all your basic needs are met, emotionally and physically, can make you less susceptible to con artists who appear to offer solutions to them but as for too much in exchange. Something that seems to meet a certain need in your life, more so basic, can seem very persuasive. One might think that he/she will notice when a person is trying to manipulate him or her but, the techniques used to persuade are very subtle, and some of the tools used are very basic; thus, we are not always conscious of them.

According to psychologist Robert Cialdini, there are six major persuasion principles, and they are not always used for bad intentions. He explains that if a person used these skills to improve others' lives, it is a good thing. If someone persuaded the other not to drink and drive, then that is a good thing.

Factors Affecting the Power and Effect of Persuasion, According To Robert Cialdini

Reciprocity

The first and most common principle affecting persuasion is reciprocity. You will find that you feel obligated to do something in return to show appreciation whenever a person does you a favor. Interestingly, this feeling is in the subconscious mind such that we are not aware of its presence. A statement such as "I owe you one" or "I am much obliged" is used to show someone that we are grateful for their assistance and hope and help them whenever needed because of something they have done for us.

A manipulator who knows these techniques can use a small favor to get you to reciprocate. Sometimes, this manipulator will look for something that you need and step in to help. In return, they will ask for something that is way out of your bracket. And because 'you are obliged,' you will reciprocate the favor. The concept of reciprocity has been used widely by companies. First, they offer free samples to customers who will then feel the need to give back by buying the item even if it does not meet the standards.

One of my friends does not accept free samples in malls, so I asked her why she does not sample the designer perfumes offered. She said, "That is how we get trapped. You sample it, and the salesperson talks you into buying it even though it is overpriced. And since you already sampled, reciprocity comes into play." That explanation made a lot of sense to me.

Of course, some people do favors for others without expecting anything in return, but you have to beware. Others are manipulative, and in the majority of us, the feeling of owing someone is a very big decision influencer.

Self-Consistency

Another principle of persuasion is self-consistency. Robert Cialdini found some people are more likely to stick with an idea or goal they committed to (verbally or in writing) because of self-image. Some people associate commitment with self-image and personality. Though there is nothing wrong with being committed, to some extent is not justified. These people who apply the principle of self-consistency can get so lost in their idea that even when it becomes invalid, they continue to honor it.

We like to present a consistent image to the world and ourselves. As such, it becomes hard to leave a thing we started even after realizing that it is not worthy.

Gradually, we develop a sense of sympathy for the idea we have been following, such that quitting is hard.

The term brainwashing is derived from a Chinese expression that means 'to wash the brain.' The concept of brainwashing became clear during the Korean War. The Chinese who were instructed to repeat certain pro-Communist and anti-American ideas to prisoners gradually began to believe their statements. A belief you practiced but did not believe gradually becomes part of you.

People who follow the lead bully often start out doing small favors and tasks. After a while, it becomes hard to leave the practice because of maintaining face in public. So, when the lead bully becomes selfish to others, the followers cannot make a different choice. Do not underestimate the power of the fear of loneliness. Do not undermine the need to be consistent and to feel. It can make a person do things he/she would not do under normal circumstances.

Social Proof

The power of social proof is something no one can deny. We are mostly herd creatures of society in many ways. As human beings, we tend to follow what others are doing. If a million people are doing a certain thing, then they cannot be wrong, so we follow them. Do you think people would wear pants that revealed their underwear if no one else was doing it? If a large number of people start to sing along some weird songs, chances are, others will join the crowd. We tend to do things done by other people.

Of course, we have to realize that there are things done by crowds with perfectly good reasons. However, there is a 'madness of the crowd' concept whereby we do not want to think for ourselves. That is a very strong persuasion tool used by manipulators and persuaders.

Perceived Authority

One powerful persuader is a confident, authoritative attitude. Have you ever walked into an office with nothing but confidence and authority and gotten what you want? Do you understand why they say confidence is very important during an interview? An authoritative manner can persuade people. Anyone will think that you have power and knowledge just because of a confident appearance.

Most of the ex-Nazis explained that they just followed the orders of their leaders. Just because someone with authority said it, then it must be correct. Titles, too, add to the perceived authority. For example, a teacher, a scientist, or a king can say anything, and it appears correct.

In the 1960s, Stanley Milgrams did experiments revealing that most people can carry out highly questionable and cruel acts so long as the person asking has the perceived authority. The problem with this [principle of perceived authority is that it can easily be faked by putting on the appropriate uniform, speaking in a certain manner, and behaving in a particular way. All of us are capable of falling for fake authority. Once again, we allow someone to think for us.

Likeability

On the face, there is nothing particularly sinister about likability. Interestingly, it has been identified as the fifth principle of persuasion. Likable people are very persuasive. Everyone can easily fall for the charm of a likable person. It has been found that people are more likely to purchase things from someone they like, and that is why many companies look for likable salespersons. Likable people are often attractive, and if they try too hard, it comes across as smarmy. However, if we truly like them, there are high chances of us purchasing things from them. In fact, how many times have you heard a person who was conned say, "but he/she seemed nice"?

The world has confirmed that attractive people are more likable, cleverer, braver, and better than plain ones. That mentality is termed as 'the Halo effect.' The challenge is, even the most attractive people might not have pure intentions towards you.

Scarcity

The fact that gold is rare makes it more interesting to find and purchase. You have heard people say that if diamonds grew on trees, no one would care about them, but now that they are rare, we value them. What makes them so precious is their scarcity – there are not many of them around. That is why offers in the malls have deadlines. It is also the reason why you hear salespeople saying, "We can only give this offer till Monday" or "This offer is valid while this stock lasts, and people are buying a lot." The thought that these items will soon be scarce will make you want to make a purchase. The perceived scarcity adds value to the product.

In the case of people, these scarcity experiences run deep and affect us more than we think. For instance, if we have a partner or spouse who is grumpy, moody, and disagreeable most of the time, we might fall into the trap of feeling extremely grateful when they display a shred of happiness. In such a case, we will be manipulated into doing things to get a glimpse of that rare happy moment. Their pleasant behavior is scarce and is, therefore, very valuable to us.

Psychologist B.F Skinner, a behaviorist, found that inconsistent rewards are more compulsive and addictive because of the scarcity. Therefore, a dog that is not always rewarded with food will act more compulsively than food used to food now and then. Unbelievable but true, if gambling involved sure wins all the time, it would not be as interesting. Maybe the person who keeps going back to the abusive relationship is just addicted to the few good times in that relationship. So, be on the safe side and stay aware of the people using the scarcity principle on you.

Beware of the people using these principles. Do not get persuaded by manipulators just because you are under the influence of scarcity or liking. Do not fall for fake authority or social proof tricks. It is okay to change if you find that something is not working as expected. If need be, lose the self-consistency and need to reciprocate.

Why Is Persuasion Important?

Why Do You Need Persuasion?

We all like to think that we are people with minds of our own. The idea of someone being able to wield power over our ability to analyze and decide for ourselves can be frightening. However, it is a basic fact of life that every decision we make is based on several different influences on our lives. We make all of our decisions based on both internal and external pressures for us to do so. We may have made up our minds in one direction, and then something happens, and we start thinking in an entirely different way. The reality is that changing our minds is a natural part of the human psyche and mastering this skill is just part of being human.

Unlike any other creation that walks this earth, humans are some of the most social of all living species. Our ability to communicate is key to our survival and is the main reason why we go to such great lengths to make sure that others understand us. We even exercise our communication skills without even thinking about them. Think about the automatic mental game your mind plays as soon as you enter a room. Immediately the brain scans the room searching for those people that we view as important to us. We look for our friends, for those who think and act as we do, and those we would hope we can build a connection to. Our minds do this instinctively; there is no planning or plotting involved, but the result is that we surround ourselves with people we'd like to influence us or those we feel confident we can influence.

Our brains divide our social connections into two camps. The first group includes those we perceive will benefit us in the future, and the second are those with whom we connect emotionally or have some common bond or goals we share.

There are many aspects in our life that require us to be persuasive:

Marketing

If you are in any business type, your ability to attract and keep customers will be directly affected by how persuasive you can be. Any business can get off to a good start with supportive friends and family members, but to give your business any kind of staying power, you'll have to convince strangers to trust in you and the products or services you offer.

Management

Another crucial aspect of your business is managing employees and getting them to follow your directions. Part of being a good manager is being able to influence another person's behavior. But the skill is not limited to business; rather, it can also be used when interacting with family members, in social circles, and a wide range of other areas of one's life. Anytime you need to motivate someone to follow your directions, you'll need persuasive speaking skills.

Teaching

A large part of teaching is influencing your students in some way or another. Whether you're teaching pre-school or at the university level, getting students to grasp your lessons and apply them to their lives will require you to have some pretty good persuasive arguments. A good teacher knows how to guide people's behavior, so you need to know how people respond to others and use that to your advantage.

Charities

Charities use persuasive speech in every aspect of their business. Their goals are to motivate people to volunteer, make donations, and to speak out against and for all sorts of causes, often without any form of compensation. A charity's success will depend largely on how effective they are in connecting with their audience emotionally and moving them to action. To do this, you need to influence people's opinions.

For Help

Whether you need someone to bag your groceries at the supermarket or you want that landlord to choose you over a hundred other tenants, it is the power of influence that will move them to do so. It is one thing to ask someone to do something for you and another entirely to persuade them to do it. Knowing how to request so people are more likely to respond can get you the help you need.

Opinions

Whether you're an environmentalist, politician, or social activist, persuasion can make you more successful.

Because persuasion is a natural part of our mental and emotional fabric, it is a key element in giving our life foundation. Everyone uses it, so whether you become a persuasion expert or not, the reality is simple. If you're not doing the persuading, the odds are quite high that you're being persuaded yourself.

Persuasion and Your Daily Life

Persuasion is unbelievable and of utmost importance in our world today.

Almost every human interaction involves an attempt to persuade or influence others to the speaker's way of thinking.

This is true regardless of professions, age, sex, philosophical beliefs, or religion.

People are always trying to convince each other.

It is undeniable that all human beings want to have the ability to persuade others, so they will hear, believe, and support them.

The people who can effectively use persuasion tactics will always find excellent employment opportunities even if the economy is experiencing problems.

If you can persuade other people, then you have a power that you can use to make your life better.

Think about every person who has influenced you to do your best and become successful in your entire life.

Persuasive people can improve lives, avoid wars, and keep adolescents free from drugs or alcohol.

However, some persuasive people can also destroy lives, start wars, and convince kids to try drugs or alcohol.

That means persuasion is a powerful ability you can use for positive or negative things, depending on your motives.

On the other hand, it would be best to use this power to increase self-improvement and overall growth for the entire community.

There are many reasons why you would want to use persuasion. It usually has something to do with convincing other people to do something that you would like. Most of us have heard about persuasion, and we associate it with things that are not always the best. For example, we may be used to seeing persuasion being used as a manipulation technique, which is only brought out when we want to force someone to act in a certain way. Or we may think of persuasion as the annoying techniques used in advertising, ones that we hear all the time and are probably really sick of.

But these are just a few examples of persuasion, and in fact, they are a little bit misleading. Persuasion is not manipulation, and, for the communication to be considered persuasion, the other party needs to have free will. You can use certain language to try and convince them that one method is better than another one, or you can try to use a little peer pressure to convince them that they should act in a specific way, but the fact remains that the other person you are talking to should have the free will to choose.

Plus, there are many good examples of how you can use persuasion to your advantage and the other person's advantage. If you go out one night to a new restaurant and love the food, it is still a form of persuasion if you try to convince the other person to visit that restaurant. If you want to see a specific movie, listing off the reasons they should come along with you can be persuasive.

There are no rules that state that the other person has to give up something or be harmed for this to be persuasion. Yes, advertising is persuasion, and it does ask the other person to give up their money and even some time to go and get the item, but not all persuasion works this way. Any time you try to convince the person to act a specific way or try to help influence their decisions, regardless of how the outcome affects you, can be considered persuasion.

Persuasion is all around us, and while we may think that we are smart enough to recognize it all of the time and make our own decisions, this is not always the case. Yes, most types of advertising are not all that convincing unless you were actively looking for a specific product and are comparing your options, but there are many times when persuasion will come into our lives, and we don't even realize that we are being persuaded to act in a certain way.

For example, if a friend tells you that there is a new place to go and have dinner some time and then asks you to come along a few weeks following, how would you respond? It is most likely unless you had made other plans ahead of time, that you would agree to go with them. You had the free will, but because this person is your friend and you value their opinion, you would likely go to the restaurant with them.

As you can see, there are many different ways that persuasion can be present in your daily life. You will find persuasion all around the place, and when you learn how to use it for yourself, rather than always letting someone else do it to you, it can make a change in how your life is going. It will help you influence your friends and family, and it will help you get the things you want out of life.

There are a lot of times when you would want to bring persuasion into your life. Some of the reasons to use persuasion include:

- To sell products: one of the most prominent places where you will see a lot of persuasions is product sales. Businesses spend billions of dollars each year trying to persuade consumers that they need them better than any other. And while some advertisements are obvious and easy to ignore, many of them are pretty advanced, and you may fall victim to persuasion if you are not careful.

- To get help with something: if you need someone to take some time out of their day to help you out, you will need to use persuasion to get them to do this. Some people will be willing to help out with it simply because you are their friend, and they like you, but sometimes you need to use some phrases and techniques to get the results.

- To convince someone to try something: any time you would like someone to try something new, whether it is a new restaurant, a show, or something else, you are using persuasion. It is often meant to be helpful; you want the other person to enjoy themselves, and you think they will like the new place.

History of Persuasion

The persuasion can be traced back to Greek origins. It was used as a tool by great orators to get their message across to the common folk. For a country that has created the political frameworks behind democracy, persuasion was immensely popular. If you have ever taken an advanced writing class that went over rhetorical analysis, you might recognize the three rhetorical modes of pathos, ethos, and logos. Aristotle billed these as the three main appeals that an orator could make to move their audience.

Its usage implies that the audience is a malleable entity, like putty. A skilled orator's words can manipulate the audience like a child might manipulate a piece of putty. Other times, persuasion is used to rile up an already popular cause, to begin with, but that had been up to that point undisclosed.

The three rhetorical modes are important because they represent three different attack vectors that a manipulator might use to persuade their audience. Again, any form of persuasion is a type of mental manipulation, but it doesn't become a psychological attack until it becomes malicious. In other words, there is a difference between plain old persuasive arguments and using persuasion to carry out dark psychology.

Regular persuasion is the type that might make you vote for a candidate or buy some product (though some would argue that modern-day advertising has dark psychology aspects). On the other hand, malicious persuasion might entice you to go against your set of morals and beliefs. This sort of persuasion is dangerous because an attacker's arguments may seem very convincing to you when, in reality, they are just cleverly designed to trick you. At the same time, the persuasion is being used to benefit someone else.

The dark psychology mindset tells us that there are people out there with less than kind objectives. They may be after your wealth, your emotional labor, your body, your mind, or just a few minutes of your attention. And all of this is theoretically possible through the levying of persuasive techniques. But first, we should talk about everyday persuasion in the traditional sense.

Modern-Day Aristotle

No matter what persuasive argument you come across, they will have all of the semblances of Aristotle's appeals, mixed in with a modern "secret sauce" that is unique to the persuader (and indeed the situation). It is still worth talking about persuasion and persuasive arguments because they are the cornerstone of all manipulation types. If a manipulator were a boxer, persuasion techniques would be like their left jab. Not as powerful as a KO punch, but still the punch that lands them the most points and slows down their opponent.

A modern-day Aristotle can be anyone. A politician, a used car salesman, even your mother is trying to convince you to move closer to home. And it is your job to decide whether their needs are genuine and desirable for all parties. They will no doubt stop at anything to convince you that they are. To do this, you have to separate their argument from the chaff. For persuasive techniques, the chaff is usually the bubbly language or the sharp edge in their arguments that cut you into you.

But beware. Just because it cuts you, it doesn't mean that it is deep or meaningful to you in any way. Many skillful persuaders will only pander to already preconceived notions that their audiences may have. They say something that they know their audience will like and instantly become that much more credible.

But someone trying to come up with a novel argument will first have to design a rhetorical strategy using any of the three rhetorical modes available. It is true whether they are trying to form an essay, a speech, or persuade you into doing something. The world of sales is chock-full of strategies used designed to get you to buy. A competent salesperson may try to get to know you first (especially if the purchase is large, like a new house or car). They wish to form a relationship on a first-name basis and then pose as a close friend.

In the world of sales, the only thing that matters is the purchase. If a client decides to buy, then whatever strategies are used to make that sale are fair. It opens the ground for deploying several different types of psychological tricks against the unsuspecting client. For example, a salesperson may introduce them to a high-end item that is purposely out of their buying range and then redirect them towards an item of similar functionality perceived as being more affordable.

A family looking to buy a new laptop for their college-bound son may be directed towards the expensive and latest Apple laptop product only to realize that it is well out of their budget. The savvy salesperson can then walk them to the Windows computers aisle and show them an alternative product that is the same color as an Apple computer but has a different operating system and is slightly less performative. Now, that other laptop may still be a flagship item and have a sizable price tag, but it is perceived as a good buy by the family because the salesperson showed them an item, they believe to be state of the art.

More psychological persuasion involves more trickery and deception—the type of things one would expect except dark psychology techniques. Indeed, the salesman's trick of going high and then going low can pass as a type of emotional manipulation. It is subtle, but there is clear pandering towards what clients believe their money can buy them. First, they are shown what is considered to be the "it" product. But since they can't afford it, the salesman puts them on an emotional roller coaster of desire.

In a way, it is a projection of what the client believes they deserve. Sure, they can't afford the best, but since they feel like they deserve the best (and since the salesman believes they deserve the best), buying the other best product is an easy choice. And if they can afford the high-end object the salesman shows them first, their job is already finished. In other words, whether the client buys the expensive item or the lesser expensive one, the salesman still wins. It is a perfect example of a psychological manipulation that is difficult to detect in the moment's heat and has a high success rate.

Models of Persuasion

If you have mastered the art of persuasion, you have garnered a multifaceted and priceless skill. Persuasion is another way of getting what you want without bleeding your victim or target individual completely dry. Successful persuasion is created by building trust between two parties, whether superficial or not, to achieve a specific goal through the act of persuasion.

The core component of persuasion is using persuasive language, a diverse method of using language, language constructs, and, if you prefer a traditional approach, rhetorical devices in speech or conversation as a persuasion method (Lamb, 2013). Although the act of persuasion generally has a singular goal, which is to persuade and get an individual to react in a certain way, there are different types of persuasion, some more sinister than others. Whichever way, it is useful to know the differences between persuasion and manipulation; manipulation has the opposite effect on individuals, which means that you won't get the desired response from your target individual or audience if you confuse the two.

Traditionally, persuasion is classified into three rhetorical categories, which are still used in academic writing today to train students in classic argumentative techniques. These persuasive techniques or rhetorical devices are known as ethos, pathos, and logos. These techniques, which the famous philosopher Aristotle taught over 2000 years ago, still have some relevance in our methods of persuasion today. Let's fly through them before focusing on the darker realm of persuasion. Firstly, ethos refers to a person's credibility when it comes to their persuasive technique. This can include "automatic" credibility that a person would have if they, for example, hold a Ph.D. in a specific field, and they are aiming to persuade you of something within that field. You are likely to believe them without question due to their qualifications, and this is an example of ethos. After, pathos relates to how effectively the attempt to persuade appeals to human emotions. If you can move a person with your persuasive tactics, then you were successful according to the concept of pathos. Finally, logos refer to persuasive tactics that appeal to an audience or a target's rational side. Facts are necessary to establish a basis on which you can build other persuasive tactics. In this case, it's best to avoid faulty logic and prepare this part of your approach, so it comes across as organized and natural ("Modes of Persuasion," 2018). As persuasive tactics developed through time to fit marketing and sales needs, and even other darker requirements, new approaches and methods have been added to ensure a foolproof approach and a high success rate.

Covert Persuasion

Covert persuasion is regarded as one of the most successful persuasive techniques by those who have studied its techniques and potential. The purpose of covert persuasion is not to be unethical or underhanded but to be so subtle that the target individual doesn't notice that these tactics are being used. And, as they say, as subtle as they are, they are also equally effective. Let's take a look at why and how this subtler-than-subtle approach is so deliciously deceptive.

The primary principle of covert persuasion is changing the perception of the "main idea" the target individual has in their mind without them realizing it. Of course, you'd want to gently nudge their ideas into the direction you want it to go, whether it is for them to become more perceptive to buying your products or using your services as a business or just to support your idea from a social perspective. One of your most powerful weapons in covert persuasion is words and how you use them (Gulyani, 2014).

When you use covert persuasion, it's important to be aware of the fact that your target's weak point is their emotions, and this is how the persuasive process starts - by playing on those emotions and steering them into a favorable direction by establishing trust, building rapport, and using words that resonate with your target. However, you can't achieve successful results using covert persuasion if you don't apply yourself to your client's situation and listen to what they say. If you listen and try to rephrase their ideas in your own words and your frame of reference, you'll better understand their point of view, which will give you a head start when it becomes your turn to speak. And, when it's your turn to speak, you can use words wisely to play on the issue you just identified by actively listening to your target. Covert persuasion is also about figuring out what will prevent your target from becoming more agreeable. For example, if you are trying to make a sales pitch to your target, it will benefit your approach if you can identify any past bad experiences they've had with sales or salespeople. You can use this "bad experience" as a tool of persuasion. Here are some of the most important covert persuasion tactics you need to know about whether you are in sales or you want to know how persuasion works so you can identify when it's happening to you (Dejan, 2020).

Persuasion and Manipulation: Know The Difference

The first and very basic indication that there is an elephantine gap between the concept of manipulation and persuasion is how people react when you label them as one or the other. For example, if you call a person a manipulator or a manipulative person, this is generally seen as an insult because people see it as an attack on their character. However, if you call someone persuasive, they may see this as a compliment. So, for some reason, even though persuasion and manipulation have a few things in common, manipulation is regarded to be different from other forms of influence and is also generally considered to be immoral.

Manipulation's bad reputation is most likely linked to its effect on the individual or group being manipulated, in contrast to those subjected to persuasive ethical tactics. As we learned, a victim of manipulation is harmed, mostly emotionally, and even advertisements and marketing can cross the line from persuasion to manipulation. However, we also know that there are instances where manipulation can be harmless, so its sinister quality lies in the intent of the manipulator and not the act of manipulation itself. Let's say, for example, a good friend was in a relationship where she was abused and treated badly, and the relationship subsequently ended. However, she wants to reconcile with her ex,

47

but those close to her know that the abuse would start again if this happens. To alienate their friend from her abusive ex, they tell her that he's been cheating on her in an attempt to make her change her mind about him, which is a dishonest, manipulative act. However, they are doing this to keep her from making the same mistake again, so do you think this is an example of malicious or immoral manipulation? (Noggle, 2018).

On the other hand, while there is a sense of duality linked to the ethics behind manipulation, communication theorists claim that persuasion should be classified as ethically neutral. What does it mean if something is regarded to be ethically neutral? Does this mean that it is or can be good? A useful way to understand the difference between persuasion and manipulation is to view persuasion as a way to align your objectives and views with those of your audience. Persuasion utilizes behavioral insights, but if it is true to its nature, it does not exploit the target audience's psychological and emotional weaknesses. The core difference between the two approaches seems to start with intent (Okoli, 2018).

After taking in all of this insightful information, there is still one dilemma. Why, if some acts of manipulation have good intent, are they still seen as manipulative and not persuasive if the key difference is the intent? The answer here is that these bona fide acts of manipulation, no matter how honorable the intent, still use manipulative tactics like dishonesty and deception, such as in the example earlier, the girl's friends deliberately deceived her by telling her a lie about her ex to protect her from further abuse. It's like comparing two white shirts to each other. One is spotless, and the other has an oil stain but is not completely spoiled.

Persuasive Techniques to Know And Use

The following techniques are squeaky clean. They work, and to master the darkness, you have to know the light. These methods and tips will help you know what to look for, how to read, and what to say to people if you want to persuade them successfully. Let's get you geared up for success.

Start a conversation by actively trying to determine how a person's mind works, what drives them and motivates them. Try to learn about the person you are engaging with and their interests, and if you don't know anything about them, show a genuine interest and fake it 'til you make it. By talking about a topic that interests the person, they will automatically lower their mental defense level. This is a classic covert technique that will help you position yourself in a space where you can connect with the person on a comfortable level. Keep in mind that this position should enable you to create change in this person's way of thinking, and this change should specifically work towards your end goal. It's a great tactic to build rapport with this person; in the end, they must feel better for having met you and feel like they gained something useful or meaningful from talking to you (Nahai, 2013; Dejan, 2020).

When you feel like you've established rapport and a sense of trust you can continue building on, you can use their perspective and motivations, along with factual information relevant to what you want them to believe, to start reframing their mindset. It can be as simple as implying their wants, mentioning the strategic shortcomings of a competitor, and including factual information that will establish a perception of superiority regarding your product in their mind. By doing this, you have created a need for them to choose not just any product, but your product (Musumano, 2017).

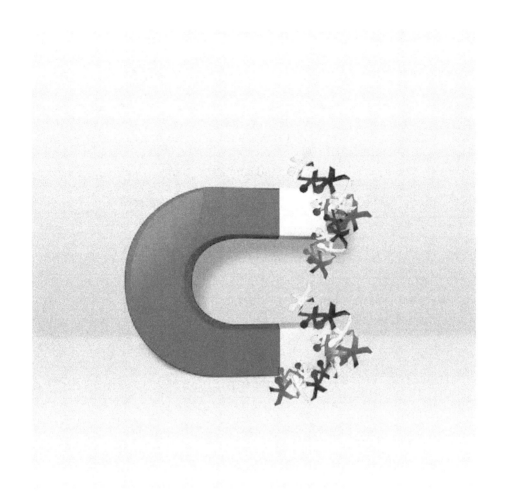

Another technique that will subtly imprint certain ideas on the individual's mind is repetition but using it wisely. By mindlessly repeating yourself over and over again, you're going to sound like one of those infomercial ads that want to sell you a dysfunctional vacuum cleaner. You can choose keywords to repeat now and then subtly, and an intelligent approach is to link these words to specific needs the individual has revealed as important to them. For example, when you apply this repetition technique to email writing, you will most likely repeat the same line or similar sentences containing keywords in your subject line, the opening part of your email, and again at the end. Try doing the same when you need to persuade someone. The trick is to make it sound authentic when you are doing it verbally and to not sound like a recording on repeat (Musumano, 2017).

Key Elements of Persuasion

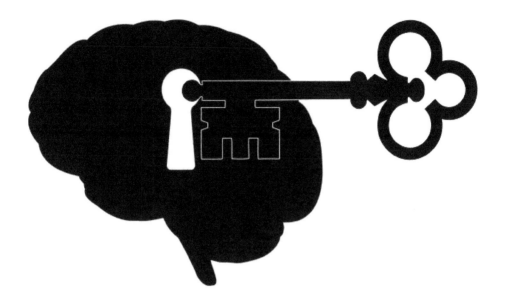

Persuasion is the ability to transmit ideas and disseminate them by those who act as recipients. This translates more effectively as the ability that human beings have through a relationship, to convince others. Persuasion is a tool that can be used in fields such as marketing, advertising, and commerce, basically sectors of the economy in which the public is sensitive to various interactions with environmental media and where the decision is the objective of who persuade

Let us elaborate on a scene where a seller wants his products to be acquired by the buy. Besides being useful, l must be attractive and, in one way or another, more desirable than that of the competition. This is achieved with persuasion, which attracts customers by offering the best product or service attributes, effectively providing comfort to the buyer by relating the most promotional aspects to the most personal. In turn, persuasion generates competition and demand in the market, generating dynamism of intentions and offers that fosters sustainable economies.

Another use of persuasion that we see in a society constantly is in the application of the law. In a trial, the lawyers and the law, as the main tool, use the elements in their favor and persuade the jury and the judge that they are valid to win the case.

We are always waiting for others who live in our environment to reproduce or share our ideas. Even unintentionally, people seek to persuade others so that their ends are fulfilled. A wife who asks her husband to optimize expenses is trying to convince him that it is the best for both. Either way, each person's ideas will be interpreted as an intention for others to apply and build their ideas based on the initial idea. Persuasion can be so extreme that it can change how a person thinks; it all depends on what the person who persuades another looks like.

To better understand the process by which one person or medium can influence another by changing their mind, it is necessary to take into account the key elements of the process, these being the issuing source, the receiver, the message itself, and the technique that It is used to transmit it.

1.   Issuer

Concerning communicating the data, the source that attempts to convince, two qualities are mulled over regarding being or not being convinced: its appeal and believability. It has appeared in different investigations that we, by and large, consider those people we see to be more solid (incompletely in light of the radiance impact, in which we accept that somebody who has a decent quality will have others). These are the reasons why people of incredible actual allure, or all-around esteemed VIPs, regularly show up in promoting to sell us an item.

Nonetheless, the most compelling component of the source regarding convincing us is believability, which is given to the source's degree of skill in the topic and the apparent genuineness.

2.   Receiver

As to the beneficiary of the message, the principal qualities that influence the hour of being affected are simply the degree of knowledge, regard, and contribution to the subject.

It must be contemplated that the knowledge level's impact ought not to be taken as an immediate measure. It isn't that who is more powerful is less astute, yet somebody with higher knowledge will have more assets to scrutinize the contentions set forward in influence. By having a higher ability to learn and use the data continuously retained, exchanging the most intelligent individuals is more liquid and reliable, reflected in the outcomes they acquire regarding persuading.

Concerning confidence, we, by and large, find that the lower confidence, the more outlandish we will think about our contentions as substantial, all the more effectively tolerating those of others.

3. **Message**

One more of the fundamental components with regards to convincing somebody is simply the message. A few investigations show that the reality of utilizing a more normal or more passionate message will rely upon the kind of reaction you need to support. It likewise influences the message consolidating components that cause dread or a feeling of danger: as indicated by Rogers's security inspiration hypothesis, we will, in general, look for and consider more certain words that permit us to limit or maintain a strategic distance from harm.

The way that influences frequently happens with a shut or open message has been examined, showing that it is commonly better to leave an end not entirely clear, albeit guided toward which one wishes to convince. This might be because this way, the audience members are more fulfilled when they arrive at those resolutions, something they experience as though it had been a revelation made without anyone else, without somebody attempting to force a thought from outside.

Persuasion Skills

First, you need to learn to recognize when you are being manipulated so you can counteract it. For this purpose, we will now look at what the experts say on how this sort of behavior can exist among us.

Are you feeling manipulated?

What then, in our everyday lives, do we need to be wary of?

Persuasive Language

The idiom that every picture tells a story is very true. Words can be so much more powerful as they inspire and encourage us, even to the point of manipulation. How many times have you been inspired by a good orator, whose daring speech motives you into action? Words even influence when we are lost completely in a great journal. The art of words can influence us to believe something, even when our eyes tell us differently. Communication is a powerful tool, especially when it comes to making people do things.

Six Theories of Psychological Manipulation

Cognitive

There are many well recognized psychological processes in theories regarding the art of persuasion. One of those is the Cognitive Response model, developed by Anthony Greenwald in 1968. It is still relevant today for determining some factors in persuasion. It is also a model used extensively in the world of advertising.

Greenwald suggested that:

It is not the message that determines the success of persuasion, but more the receiver's emotions. The internal monologue of the one receiving the message will decide how easily they are influenced. Such internal thoughts will include positive and negative aspects, according to the individual's personality. This not a learning process, but more based on whether the person already views the message with favorable or unfavorable thought processes (cognition).

Overcoming any counter-arguments will rely on the expertise of the persuader. They should stop their target from having sufficient time to construct any counter-arguments. The persuader must encourage positive arguments to come to the forefront. This gives the "persuasion effect" a better chance of success.

Persuasion can be more difficult if the intended target has been forewarned. It allows the target time to build counterarguments if the "message" is counter-intuitive to their present cognitions. The importance of pre-warning can be seen in research conducted by Richard E. Petty in 1977. The study showed that students given notice about a certain event were less likely to be persuaded than those who had no pre-warning.

Reciprocity

Another well-studied explanation for how we might be open to the power of persuasion is the Rule of Reciprocity. This is based on a principle related to social conventions. If someone does you a favor or does something good for you, you will be more likely to feel obliged to return the favor.

The Rule of Reciprocity can also happen subconsciously. Without even realizing it, you may agree to action, or favor asked of you by the requester. All because at some point, they had done something for you, and you feel in their debt. You may feel obliged even if the request is something you would normally decline.

It is an effect widely used by companies who are looking to make sales. Often companies give out free samples or time-limited trials. This is not without a motive. It is hoping that the customer feels obliged to return the favor and buy the product or continue with the agreement.

Reciprocity is a recognized psychological process. It is an adaptive behavior that would have increased our chances of survival in the past. By helping others, it is likely that at some following point, they will help you. However, it can also have negative effects. If someone does something bad to you, you may be driven by reciprocity rules to exact your revenge.

The Rule of Reciprocity is well supported by academic research. Burger et al. (2009) suggested that a group of participants were more likely to agree to a request if the requester had partly done them a favor.

Information Manipulation

A powerful tool in the manipulator's armory. This is a method of being outright deceitful. It is a means of providing limited and confusing information to the victim. The effect of this will unbalance their way of thinking, making them vulnerable. It can also incorporate the use of intentional body language to persuade and manipulate someone.

A study by McCornack et al. (1992) showed the different ways a message can be falsified to assist in the manipulation process. McCornack's theory has a premise of four maxims in a truthful statement. A breach of any of these will render the message as intentionally deceitful. The four maxims are:

Quantity

This is the "amount" of information provided. Most of us seek to provide the right amount of information so that the receiver understands our message. Not too little, or too much, as that might confuse. A manipulator, though, would play with that quantity of information. They may omit certain pieces they consider irrelevant most, especially if it is likely to work against their argument. This is known as "lying by omission."

Quality

Refers to the "accuracy" of the information provided. Truthful communication is one of High Quality. If we were to violate this maxim, then the receiver hears intentional mistruths. This is "outright lying" to gain the manipulator's power.

Relation

Here, we talk about the "relevance" of the information to the message. To confuse or sidestep an awkward question, the manipulator may go off-topic. This is a way of changing the subject for the sole purpose of misleading. It could be to hide their weaknesses. Or even to over-emphasize something that will give them more power over their listener.

Manner

The "presentation" of the message. An important aspect of this is body language. We read inflections and facial expressions as we listen. A manipulator may exaggerate these to mislead the presentation of the message. This is all in the aim to emphasize their agenda.

Lying to manipulate or persuade someone is not a new concept. It is, though, a method that is becoming particularly potent in the modern world. Online communication and social media do not always involve face-to-face contact. This makes it easier to tell mistruths or exaggerate information. A manipulator may work in their elements with such communications.

Nudge

Not all manipulation is sinister. Sometimes we may be manipulated to help us make the right decisions for our good. To do this, the Nudge Theory is particularly useful. The Nudge Theory expands positive reinforcement by using small nudges.

Skinner's studies, or behaviorism, show how useful this theory can be. Positive reinforcement, such as rewards, can manipulate people into behaving in the manner you are hoping to encourage.

One example of "nudging" can be seen in this example. Adding exceptionally high-priced items on a menu may seem counterproductive. Yet, the result of this increased the sales of the second highest-priced item. The customers were given a "nudge" in the right direction, but for the restauranteur's benefit.

Richard Thaler, considered the Nudge Theory father, was awarded the Nobel Memorial Prize in Economic Sciences. His contribution to behavioral economics was considered quite momentous. Nudge Theory gives positive reinforcement, or as Thaler described it, it gives "nudges."

The Nudge Theory is not only effective in economics. It can be used to encourage behavioral changes and to influence personal choices. Even accepted social norms can be manipulated to changes in this way.

Nudging is so successful that in 2010 the British Government set up a Department Behavioral Insights Team. This was to help develop policies. The department was referred to as the Nudge Unit.

There can be obvious benefits of using "nudges" to influence people. It is still a form of psychological manipulation that can infringe on an individual's civil liberties.

Social Manipulation

This type of manipulation is also known as psychological manipulation. It is often a tool for politicians or other powerful people who are used to advancing their interests. In its worst form, it is a means of social control. By taking away individuality, it coerces the populace into accepting what is given to them. Though it can have a positive side when used to help with personal issues, such as improving health and wellbeing.

Those in power who use social manipulation may use destructive techniques to deflect from important issues. They would argue that their proposals are for the benefit of the populace and the benefit of your family and its future. Anything you think personally that might be different is wrong and selfish. This type of persuasion is very paternalistic, almost treating individuals as if they were all children. This "system" will strive to make the crowds believe the things that have gone wrong are, in fact, their fault. The only way to resolve the problem is to listen to the guidance of those who know better.

Such a political strategy would bring to the forefront one social problem, only to hide another. It is a tactic to cause social unrest and panic among the populace. By creating unease in society, the populace will begin to demand changes. An example could be that the department wishes to hide the problems of health care. So, they decrease the budget in crime prevention, causing crime statistics to rocket. The populace will receive information to coerce them into believing the best way forward for the crime problem. The politicians will feed propaganda by disseminating their truths and facts. It may not always be true, or it may be information that is exaggerated, such as misuse of statistics. This type of social manipulation could take years to get the result that the manipulator requires.

The use of psychological manipulation is all a part of social influence. Professor Preston Ni, Communication Studies, published an article in Psychology Today. He indicates that one party recognizes another's weaknesses. They deliberately set out to cause an imbalance of power. This enables them to exploit their victims for their agenda.

Gaslighting

This is perhaps the cruelest form of manipulation. It is a means of casting into doubt the sanity and self-esteem of a person. You could say it is sowing the seeds of doubt into the victim of manipulation. Working on a similar principle such as "knowing you are being told repeated lies." Until eventually, you begin to believe the lies as the truth.

It is an unkind form of manipulation. The gas-lighter will cause their victim to lose all confidence in their credibility. This leads to destroying their self-worth. All because they begin to doubt themselves. That is the intention of gaslighting to reduce the victim to a psychological mess. The manipulator will constantly put their target down by contradicting them. Also, by convincing them that they are always wrong. Sometimes to the point that the victim will be accused of telling lies. This is why the victim loses all self-esteem. When that happens, they become ruled by the domineering influencer. It is a form of mental abuse, often seen in abusive personal relationships. The influencer will use constant techniques to make their victim doubt. Even to the point of doubting their memories by denying things they've said and done.

How to Influence People?

Brainwashing

Brainwashing doesn't come easily and could take quite a lot of time to be effective. This phase is most likely to concentrate on the procedure of indoctrination as well as all the elements that feature it. Many individuals see persuading as a wicked method done by those attempting to corrupt, impact, and get power with the media and the flicks seen. Some that rely on the power of indoctrination think that individuals around them are attempting to regulate their minds and habits.

Generally, the indoctrination procedure takes place in a far more advanced method and does not include the threatening methods most individuals connect with. This phase will certainly enter into a lot of even more information concerning what indoctrination is and how it can affect the topic's mindset.

Hypnosis

Hypnosis is the after a type of dark psychology I'll be revealing. There are a whole lot of definitions of what hypnosis is. The American Psychological Association explains hypnosis as a supportive interface where the hypnotist provides suggestions to which the participant can respond. However, it becomes dark psychology when the hypnotist starts making suggestions that can harm or change the participant's acts in their environs.

Most people who undergo hypnosis allude it to a sleep-like trance kind of state. However, the hypnosis participant is in vivid fantasies, sensitive suggestibility, and focused awareness. This new-fangled state makes them more vulnerable to the recommendations that the hypnotist supplies them with.

Nonetheless, most experts agree that the effect of hypnosis as a part of dark psychology is not a reality. Although it is possible to convince the mind to accept a few changes in the subject, it is not likely that the subject can change their whole thinking system through this system. Many certified psychological professionals use this medium to assist the subject towards pain management and self-improvement rather than controlling their minds.

Manipulation

One of the top-ranking types of dark psychology that can control how a person thinks is manipulation. Psychological manipulation is a type of social influence that works to influence the decision of others. It embraces an abusive, underhanded, and deceptive approach to advance the interest of the one manipulating and those being manipulated. While most people recognize when they have been manipulated, they fail to realize that it is a kind of mind control. Manipulation could be very difficult to do away with since it occurs between people who know each other very well.

Manipulations cause the subject not to have a choice in a matter. Their minds are laced with half-truth and outright lies that leave them oblivious of the whole situation until it becomes too late. When they detect things ahead of time, they are being blackmailed by the agent to get their goals finally. The subject remains stuck in between the matter because they'll take the blame eventually if things go haywire.

Persuasion

Another form of dark psychology that works similarly to manipulation is persuasion. This part influences the motivations, behaviors, intentions, beliefs, and attitudes of the subject. Persuasion could be used for various things in our everyday life to affect a necessary form of communication to get people with contradictory ideas to agree. During this process, either spoken or written, words are used for conveying reasoning, feelings, or information to the other party.

There are a lot of different kinds of persuasion that are available. They don't all have an evil intent; however, they all work to change the subject's mind about something. A political candidate comes on TV to try to make the voter or subject vote for a particular person on the election day. The TV or online advert tries to make a subject buy a particular product. These are all types of persuasion bent on changing the thought pattern of the subject.

Deception

Deception can be considered a form of dark psychology that influences the subject's beliefs with either untrue or partial truths about things and events. However, deception could be anything ranging from propaganda, dissimulation, hand sleight, distractions, concealment, or even camouflage. Deception is a serious type of a dark psychology system that could be overly dangerous to the victim, as he or she might not be aware of the dark psychology that is going on. The victim is convinced beyond every necessary doubt that what is being said is nothing but the truth, while the opposite is the case. Deceit could be more dangerous should the concealed information be liable to make the subject prone to danger.

However, the moment the subject starts detecting or detects the agent's motive as deceit all along, they start having trouble trusting that person in future dealings. Nonetheless, deception isn't always laced with evil motives. It could be targeted at keeping a relationship from breaking off.

Methods of Persuasion

idea   planning   strategy   success

<u>*Win-Win Concept*</u>

When discussing persuasion, it is important to describe the win-win concept, which can be translated with the expression "win I - win you" put in place by the persuader. It indicates that both sides achieve a goal that both will benefit from in a situation. It is a concept behind persuasion. This is the case of honest sellers who explain the fundamental characteristics of the product they want to sell, which will serve the person who wants to sell it. "You buy this spacious and sturdy

machine that you need for your work and your large family, and I make money."
They both get something, and nobody loses!

We also find persuasion on TV in commercials, for example, which is made to attract our attention and change our minds about a specific type of product or service. This also happens outside the TV screens; we can see it on billboards or in shop windows while walking around the city.

Build Your Trust

You can't pretend to master the art of persuasion unless you're sure of yourself, what you're doing, and what you're saying. Your audience needs to be able to sense your safety. How can you expect someone to believe what you're saying if you have doubts about it yourself? No matter how competent you are, if your target audience doesn't perceive your safety, you will most likely lose the fight and be unable to convince them.

Intensity

The word 'intensity' in this case refers to verbal language. A study has shown that subjects subject to speeches containing "strong" words, used to support the description of a product or service, are more inclined to purchase that product. This concept is also very valid in political speeches to gather more consensus among the voters. Using strong language is one of the most effective persuasive strategies that exist.

To Select

You have to select the people to reach with persuasion by identifying those interested in our goal and letting go of those who would not get involved because spending time trying to persuade these people would mean wasting time. This is especially true for marketing when you need to target the public.

Mystery

Creating a little suspense always helps persuade because it is very curious, be it, man or woman. For example, if you want to convince your friend to go to a new place, you can intrigue him. They will almost certainly follow you.

Shortage

This is a very effective technique for selling a product. Making people believe that an article is present in small quantities leads them to buy it.

Perceived Value

This, too, like the past ones, is a technique widely used in marketing. In short, it consists of persuading the customer that what he should buy is worth more than the actual value of it.

Be A Good Person

It consists of accompanying the persuasive action with a beneficial action, that is, with something that produces help for someone else. This is because doing good often produces a sense of happiness.

Make It Clear What They're Missing

This persuasive technique leverages fear, in this case, the fear of losing something, and is obtained by showing the potential buyer what he risks losing if he does not buy a product or service.

Be an Observer

You can't go anywhere if you don't pay attention to the surrounding environment, the situation, or, above all, the person you're trying to persuade. Mood, behavior, and situation must be appropriate for the time being for makeup to be effective. Remember how to read body language and know how to read this person before manipulating him into anything. If you are not paying attention to the passion and attention needed to make the trick work, you will be captured, and your success is unlikely. Attention and observation are the keys to manipulation.

Honesty and Reliability

Nobody will follow the advice or suggestions of someone they don't trust. Even if the situation does not require a relationship or a pre-developed relationship, you must appear reliable. Remember the indicators of discomfort and lying when it comes to body language and avoid them when you speak. If you are half-telling the truth or even lying to get what you want from someone, you can't do it by holding your hands behind your back and shifting the weight from one foot to another.

Get Over Your Idea

A tactic often used in the sales sector is to use intense passion to promote the idea which you want to sell to someone. It is a common practice seen by anyone who tries to sell a product, and it works. If you want someone to donate to your favorite organization, tell them that they will benefit as much as the organization will help. Prepare them to follow them before they even know what you want to offer. This technique works well when you want someone to take something, which is why it is taught to all salespeople and used in advertisements. It also works well with the opposite technique, which oversimplifies the idea.

Oversimplify Your Idea

If the idea is complicated and has disadvantages, it may be helpful to oversimplify it. By definition, excessive simplification consists of leaving out information and simplifying what is included until it is distorted. To do this via persuasion, edit what you should explain when it comes to your idea.

Put Yourself in A Neutral Position

If possible, maintain the illusion of neutrality and limit any perceived prejudice. For example, if your friend's girlfriend begged him to cut his hair for a while, then look at you for a second opinion, you shouldn't express any real interest. If you have an issue with his hair's length, you could say that you don't care in both cases. However, the length indicated in his girlfriend's photo would frame his face well, and in the after hot climate, he will avoid the possible stroke heat. The use of words with specific reactions helps. In this case, the word "anyway" causes people to focus more on what was said after than what was said before. By introducing logical points and acting as if your opinion was completely for no reason, your friend will likely choose the hairstyle, and his girlfriend may even owe you a favor.

Change the Environment to Your Advantage

Studies have shown that the environment someone is in can have an impact on their decisions. This would come as a form of subliminal persuasion. For example, if you desperately need a study partner for an upcoming exam, you shouldn't ask your favorite partner in the mall. The mall is surrounded by fun activities, bright lights, music, and other distractions. However, if I asked him in an environment that stimulates the idea of studying in his brain, such as the library, he is more likely to agree with you.

Speak Quickly

If you get involved in a discussion that you plan to win, speed up your speech. If you speak quickly, you seem more prepared with the arguments, and your opponent has less time to think about a coherent answer since he focuses on countering your arguments instead. The other person will fidget and confuse their points. Eventually, they will drop their share of the disagreement out of frustration, and you will emerge victoriously.

Creating Needs

One of the best methods of persuasion is to create a need or to reassure an old need. This question of need is related to self-protection and compatibility with basic emotions such as love. This technique is one of the biggest trumps of marketers in particular. They try to sell their products or services using this technique. The kind of approach that expresses the purchase of a product to make one feel safe or loved is part of the need-building technique.

Touching Social Needs

The basis of touching social needs is popular, having prestige, or having the same status as others. Advertisements on television are ideal examples of this. People who buy the products in these advertisements think they will be like the person in the advertisement or be as prestigious. The main reason why persuasion techniques such as touching social needs are effective is related to television advertising. Many people watch television for at least 1-2 hours a day and encounter these advertisements.

Use of Meaningful and Positive Words

Sometimes it is necessary to use magic words to be convincing. These magic words are meaningful and positive. Advertisers know these positive and meaningful words intimately. They need to be able to use them. The words "new," "renewed," "all-natural," and "most effective" are the most appropriate examples of these magic words. Using these words, advertisers try to promote their products, making the advertisements more convincing for people to like the products.

Use of Foot Technique

This technique is frequently used in the context of persuasion techniques. The processing method is quite simple. You make a person do something very small first because you think they can't refuse it. Once the other person has done so, you will try to get him to do more, provided he is consistent within himself.

Use of Orientation from Big to Small

The tendency to ask from big to small things is the exact opposite of the technique of putting a foot in the door. The salesperson makes an unrealistic request from the other person. Naturally, this demand doesn't correspond with the real issue. However, the salesperson then makes a request that is smaller than before. People feel responsible for such approaches, and they will accept the offer. Since the request is small, by accepting it, people have the idea that they will help the salespeople, and the technique of moving from big to small requests works.

Use of Reciprocity

Reciprocity is a term for the mutual progress of a business. When a person does you a kindness, you feel the need to do him a favor. This is one example of reciprocity. For example, if someone bought you a gift on your birthday, you would try to pay back that gesture. This is more of a psychological approach because people don't forget the person who does something for them, and they try to respond accordingly.

For marketers, the situation is slightly different from a human relations point of view. Reciprocity takes place here in the form of a marketer offering you an interim extra discount or "extra" promotion. You are very close to buying the product introduced by the marketer you think is giving a special offer.

Limitation Technique

The restriction technique is one of the most powerful methods to influence human psychology. You can see this mostly in places selling products. For example, if a store has a discount on a particular product, it may limit it to 500 products. This limitation can be a true limitation or a part of the limitation technique. So, you think that you will not find the product at that price again and you agree to buy that product at the specified price.

Principles of Persuasion

Reciprocity is one of the major forms of persuasion. It is about the feeling of needing to return something when something is given to you. If you invite someone over to your house, they will feel the need to invite you to their home afterward. When you compliment someone, you can see that people will normally compliment you as well.

If you want to get something from someone else, try to offer them something similar first. It can be as simple as trying their food at a restaurant. After a time, the server brings out two plates, offering your date a bite of your dish. They will likely end up offering you a bite as well.

Scarcity is the second principle. If you make yourself unavailable, then you will become even more desired. Scarcity is a tactic that many people use for online dating. They think that if they rarely respond, they will make themselves more desirable, and the other person will try even harder to mend the relationship. This result is certainly true in some cases, but people will get bored and move along, so make sure you are still giving the people what they want.

Think of one of your favorite brands. At one point in time, the company probably came out with a "limited edition" item. This release is more often than not just a marketing tactic to try and get many buyers all at once. Sometimes limited-edition items become popular enough that they become staples, and the company probably just used the "limited" status as a way to test out their product.

Scarcity is also used when people say that they only have a few items or spaces left. If you are a hairstylist, you might tell your clients to make their appointments quickly because you only have a few spots open. Many people will feel the pressure to schedule, so they will make an appointment even though they might not have been considering doing so partly. If you want to be persuasive, try using this tactic to help you get what you want.

Authority is important in persuasion, but it cannot be confused or misconstrued. Some people assume that authority comes with power and that power equals strength. Many people will yell, scream, fight, and be angry in an attempt to look as though they have authority over others. This tactic can work, but not in a respectable way.

In terms of persuasion and influence, authority refers to someone's credentials. A person will use their past certifications, training, college degrees, and other forms of quantifiable authenticity to prove their credentials. You will hear people say, "I'm a doctor," when describing a health product, which gives them the authority to decide that it is good for your health.

You will often see kinds of toothpaste marketed as "the toothpaste your dentist uses" or something along those lines as an attempt to give authority over your decision. If you want to use this persuasive principle, try finding what your authority might be. If you are interviewing for a position, you might mention that you are a college graduate or a pre-med student to help remind those who hold more power than you do to have a level of authority.

Consistency is crucial for anyone who wants to have persuasion over others. We have already talked about consistency for other reasons, but it is important to know that it is crucial to becoming a persuasive individual.

Consistency is a good skill to have because it makes people comfortable with you. If you are erratic, it can make you seem unapproachable, unrelatable, and somewhat scary.

To use consistency as a form of influence, ensure that you are sticking to your morals, beliefs, and overall identifying factors. Also, find a balance so that you do not become too predictable. If you become a too predictable person, you will not have as much influence over people, resulting in less persuasion.

Being liked is an important aspect for those who want to be persuasive. The most liked people are those who give compliments, cooperate, and are relatable. Figuring out how to be liked is challenging, and it is something that triggers us back to junior high when we were hoping not to be the last call when picking teams.

Being liked as an adult can be easier because most of us are more forgiving and less judgmental and harsh than we were in our younger years. The most liked people are those who are complimentary. However, you do not want to be someone who gives people compliments too often. It can make you seem desperate for approval, which will make you less trustworthy and not as talented in persuasion.

Still, compliments help win over the other person. Make sure your compliments are natural. Do not just give compliments because you are trying to be persuasive, or people will catch on and call you out for your phony behavior.

Others like people who can cooperate. If you show that you are willing to help out, people will be much more likely to listen to you. When you can collaborate and compromise with many different people, it shows that you are someone with whom it is easy to get along, which will lead you to become a person who can easily influence others. When you are relatable, you seem more approachable as well.

For people who are the biggest influencers, relatability is huge. Those you are trying to persuade want to see themselves in your shoes. When they can look at you and find moments of connection, they will be much easier to persuade.

When it comes to persuasion, the consensus is the last thing others will consider. They will make as many informed decisions as possible on their own, but when all else fails, they will look at what everyone else thinks before making their final decision.

For businesses, people will go online and look at reviews to determine if they want to give you their money or not. On a more personal level, people might ask their friends if they know you to get a sense of whether they should like you. Though it is important to connect with the person you are persuading, to be a good influencer, you also want to make sure that the consensus agrees on your likability and credibility.

The Concepts That Make It Work

The amplification theory is another concept that allows persuasion to work. If you build something up, people are more likely to be persuaded. This technique can work if you amplify something negatively as well.

Making someone feel bad about something they like to prove your point or give yourself validation can work, but why would you want to use this strategy? You will initially influence people, but if you continue to make others feel bad about their decisions, they will eventually look to someone else.

Asking for something small is another good concept in helping you get what you want following. If you want to persuade someone to let you borrow a hundred dollars, for example, you might first ask if you can borrow twenty. It is as if you have eased them into asking for the bigger favor following on.

Alternatively, ask for something so ridiculous that they say yes to your second request. If you ask them to dog sit for a month, many people will oppose the thought. If you then ask them to dog sit just for the weekend, they are much more likely to say yes.

Anchoring is a technique that makes someone else think they are getting away with a great deal. Stores like Kohl's and Macy's seem like they are always having some sort of sale. They use anchoring as a method to get you to buy their clothes.

Stores plan sales because they know that the illusion of saving money is what gets people to spend their cash.

You can use this method of anchoring as a persuasion tactic as well. When working with a client, if you know it takes you five days to complete a project, you might tell them you need seven. That way, you work hard to get it done in four days, and they are impressed.

In persuasion, relatability and unity are also important. We look at celebrities and wonder where their level of relatability is. Ultimately, they seem like they are perfect, but the top influencers are the ones who are not afraid to be vulnerable.

They will show pictures of themselves, not looking at their best, or share moments when they feel a little down to seem more relatable to their fans. They still don't share all the dirty details, but they have given enough away to keep people coming back because they seem so relatable.

The Ultimate Guide to Enhance your Persuasion Techniques

The energy of persuasion can open doors for you and develop the road to good results much smoother. Probably the most effective methods have the origins of their NLP (neuro-linguistic programming). These persuasion methods are derived from empathy - to persuade someone - you have to comprehend them.

Empathy-Based Persuasive Techniques

The very first and most significant thing you have to comprehend about the individual you're attempting to influence is precisely what the brain of their best response to - feel, visual, or maybe auditory stimulation. Knowing this can enable you to be persuasive by plugging into and feeding this particular desire.

Females generally respond better to feelings. However, not. Guys frequently respond very well to visuals, and several individuals are impacted by audio. To discover, and that is the very best stimulation to focus on your persuasion, look at the way they talk. Can they say, "I see," "I hear what you are saying," or maybe "I feel that."? These are obvious examples; of course, the appropriate answer might be far more subtle and maybe a blend of two kinds of stimulation.

Alter the persuasion methods of yours depending on the mind type you're offering; for instance, when persuading somebody who's "feel" orientated, focus on how they will feel if they do what you're attempting to persuade them to. Do not attempt to tell them just what it will be like - you've to make them believe it. The more you are conscious of the individual you are coping with, the more efficiently you will focus on your persuasive strategies.

Mirror Based Persuasive Techniques

Matching the body language of yours, as well as your pose/position, is a subtle but amazingly effective persuasive method. You have to be subtle, which might feel uncomfortable initially; however, with a bit of exercise, you will see just how helpful this particular method, referred to as "mirroring," may create a rapport easing persuasion.

Along with focusing the content of your persuasion in a means that interacts nicely with the specific character style of theirs, you can also correct your language and how you talk to place yourself on the Stage of theirs. Individuals react much better to persuasive strategies that are in their own "language" of theirs. Pick up on certain words they utilize as well as add them back on them, particularly adjectives. Consider their response, volume, pitch, and speed as similarly as you possibly can.

Other Persuasive Techniques

You will find a lot of different persuasive methods that you can focus on and build up. We suggest you learn the empathy/mirror effective methods, most notably, as these are the best. Nevertheless, the following methods may be useful additions to the persuasion armory yours.

- **Persuasive Words**

There are lots of subconscious persuasive words that an individual may make use of. Frequently these will be a call to action: for instance, "Do that" or perhaps "Be this." Kind words as well as adjectives, for example, "Definitely," "Most," as well as "Effective," are extremely persuasive all on their very own.

Utilize "now" words, including "today" or perhaps "at the moment" frequently to subliminally recommend urgency.

- **Rhetorical Questions**

Allowing the individual to believe for themselves is extremely motivating and can, therefore, be incredibly persuasive. Ask questions that engage them, and they are instantly open. This will even enable you to know more about them. Frequently this will persuade them they're making the decision when in reality, you've just steered them to this particular persuasion.

- **Eye Contact**

It's highly crucial to produce a great rapport with the individual you're attempting to persuade. Without eye contact, this is practically impossible. With non-threatening and consistent eye contact, you can develop trust. Include a real smile, plus persuasion will get so much easier.

Be Persuasive by Connecting Emotionally, Not Rationally

Anybody of legislative issues will tell you - people simply don't answer judiciously. They respond depending on sentiments. To convince someone, you ought to associate with them inwardly. Aristotle decided the three central parts of each enticing contention:

Ethos: the believability, information, mastery, authority, and height of the individual endeavoring to convince.

Logos: the allure of rationale, reason, psychological reasoning, realities, and information.

Poignancy: the appeal to the feelings; the non-psychological, non-thinking inspirations affect activities just as decisions.

All layers are, obviously, vital. However, it's likely the mental Stage which keeps presumably the most energy of influence. We're mental creatures and are significantly more adept at being convinced by the guarantee of feeling extraordinary rather than the guarantee of "something being right."

The Moral Behind Persuasion Techniques

You may be reasoning that utilizing influence techniques is unethical, underhand. You may wind up with the problem of whether to use them on somebody you appreciate. In reality, it is up to you precisely how you consider utilizing viable techniques yet recall the accompanying. People must be aware of the systems and comprehend when others are endeavoring to control them. If you viably convince someone, you've recently out contended them.

Influence is discretionary. After training, that is definitely, and you may find that these compelling strategies are embedded into the elements. Might you feel regretful for utilizing different components of the uniqueness of yours, such as talking unquestionably? A ton of the time, you'll be endeavoring to do what's generally valuable for these individuals in any case. The objective of interfacing with somebody mentally is to realize what they need. At whatever point you understand this, you're simply convincing them to accomplish something which they will need to do in any case. Thus, by its meaning, influence isn't controlled - it's just bringing the purpose of yours over.

People must be satisfied to settle on their own decisions. In a perfect world, you should be certain to utilize these powerful strategies to do what's suitable for those concerned.

The intensity of Conscious Persuasion

The way into the universe is the strength of influence. Influence is the one key component to getting all you require, getting rich, and accomplishing whatever. With no influence, nothing completes. It's tied in with convincing yourself as well as other people. Influence is tied in with moving cognizance, and once you can move awareness, you can move something of the universe.

All influence is convincing to make a move, regardless of whether physical or mental exercise. Best and affluent people are experts of influence. You may have had specific ideas against utilizing influence since you feel it's controlled. In any case, they're restricting convictions that you have that are keeping you from accomplishment. The usage of influence for illegitimate reasons for existing controls. However, the normal utilization of influence is really for direction. Customers wish to be guided in a way that makes them agreeable and anxious to make a move to support themselves. We all need to be driven into doing what is superb for us by somebody who could show us the way.

Understanding that notion generates reality. Persuasion is all about changing the perception of individuals to change the reality theirs. It's about helping others to see things in a diverse way that they did not see before. To make use of persuasion, you initially need to persuade yourself about the usage of persuasion. You've to change the perception of yours of persuasion. If you can shift your beliefs and perception about truth to successful and wealthy people, you can utilize the strength of persuasion in the manner they put it to use.

Probably the most powerful as well as important individuals on the planet are the persuaders. They have the potential to shift people's perceptions, choices, and beliefs about things. If you would like to alter the planet, you've to alter the consciousness of individuals. The most effective persuasion is persuasion that moves individuals to the path they currently wish to go. It's persuasion to show them the ways of getting that which they wish. You can persuade men and women to do something if they believe it is going to satisfy them. In full persuasion, the objective is persuading individuals they have a particular desire, exactly how they can satisfy that motivation, and that it's worth whatever they provide in exchange for that that will meet the desire of theirs.

Numerous locations teach persuasion in different ways; however, the basic concepts all come right down to a couple of representing all of them. It's about getting attention and sparking curiosity and interest. In that case, it's related to arousing desire and convincing them to take a particular action to fulfill that desire. The crucial point that all persuasion deals with is convincing others about the importance of something. Something just has greatly based on the importance which you give it. Who's saying that a specific product is worth a specific amount of cash? The fact is that everything in the universe is free. All of the items in life obtain their worth from the perception of individuals. The perception of worth can differ from one individual to yet another. You can develop some worth in anything merely by the way you cause others to perceive it.

Nothing in the universe is actually of any use to any being except by the consciousness that the being has towards it. All drugs medications wouldn't do the job to heal whether an individual thinks that they wouldn't heal, and their consciousness isn't in harmony for healing but illness. For an individual with the consciousness and trust for healing, a placebo would procure the outcome of healing. Nobody can get pleasure from anything until they have the consciousness to get satisfaction from that thing.

It's persuasion that makes the world go round. When individuals aren't persuaded to do anything, there'd be no movement of energy. There'd be no buying or even selling. When materials aren't being moved around, things can't be placed into the hands of those who could place them to use more effectively. The economy comes to a standstill when cash isn't flowing. When individuals keep what they've rather than offer to get something far more, it'll just lead to stagnation, entropy, and the universe's degrading.

That's why the entrepreneurs and sales promoters are doing society a huge service. By convincing individuals to see value in food and offer something different, whether it's time, information, or money to get it, they're encouraging power exchange. When power is replaced, that's when there could be experienced types and brand-new combinations of energy designed for the majority around the globe to benefit from. The exchange of electrical power is the thing that supports the evolution of humanity and also the improvement of living.

9 SECRETS TO STOP BEING MANIPULATED

1. Trust your instincts

While your brain interprets signals based on facts, logic, and sometimes experience, your heart works in the opposite direction by screening information through an emotional filter. The only thing that picks up vibrations is your gut instinct, which neither the heart nor the brain can pick on.

And if you can get to the point when you recognize your inner voice and are trained to react to it, you will lower the chances of being seduced by people trying to work on you with their manipulative will.

To begin with, it's hard to recognize this voice. And that's because you have allowed voices of doubt, self-discrimination as well as the critics ' loud voices within and without to drown out your authentic voice over the course of your life.

Your survival depends on this voice or instinct. So, trust that when it kicks in, your brain neurons can still process things in your immediate vicinity.

Some people call it intuition, and some refer to it as instinct, especially when it comes to relationships, they are undoubtedly the same thing. You must accept that it may not always make logical sense to start trusting your instincts.

If you've ever been in the middle of doing something and experienced the feeling of being watched all of a sudden, then you know what I mean. You don't have eyes at the back of your head, there's no one else with you in the room, but you get the tiny shiver running down your spine and the "sudden knowledge" someone is watching. That's what I'm talking about.

The first step to connect with your instinct is to decode your mind with the voices you've let in. With meditation, you can do this. Forget the chatter of "he said, she said." Concentrate on your center. You are the voice you know. Next, be careful about your thoughts. Don't just throw away the eclectic monologs in your head. Rather go with the flow of your thoughts.

Why do you think of a certain person in some way? How do you feel so deeply about this person, even if you only know each other for a few days? What's that nagging feeling about this other person that you have? You get more tuned to your intuition as you explore your thoughts and understand when your instincts kick and how to react to them.

You may need to learn to take a step back to pause and think if you are the kind of person who prefers to make spur decisions at the moment.

This moment in which you pause gives you the opportunity to really reflect on your decisions and evaluate them. The next part is a hard part, and it can't be followed by many people. Unfortunately, you can't skip or navigate around this step.

This part has to do with trust. You need to be open to the idea of trusting yourself and trusting others to be able to trust your instinct. Your failure to trust others would just make you paranoid, and it's not your instincts that kick when you're paranoid.

It's the fear of you. Fear tends to turn every molehill into a hill. You must let go of your fear, embrace confidence, and let that lead in your new relationships.

You are better able to hear the voice inside without the roadblocks put up by fear in your mind. Finally, your priorities need to be reevaluated.

If your mind is at the forefront of money and material possessions, you may not be able to see the past. Any interaction you have with people would be interpreted as people trying to take advantage of you, and if you dwell on that frequently enough, it will soon become your reality.

You know the law of attraction. You attract into your life what you think of. If you're constantly thinking about material wealth, you're only going to attract people who think like you. Using this as a guide, look at all your relationships with this new hindsight; the old, the new, and the perspective.

Don't enter a relationship that expects to be played. Be open when you approach them, whether it's a business relationship, a romantic relationship or even a regular acquaintance. You can get the right feedback about them from your intuition.

Do not step into this thinking, too, that your gut will tell you to run in the opposite direction when you meet people you are not sure of.

2. Practice Saying No

No is a powerful word we don't use nearly enough. There are some gender differences here as well, with women being more likely to struggle with no. Often, women have internalized cultural lessons where saying no is perceived as rude, unhelpful and selfish. That of course is absolutely not true. In fact, there is nothing wrong with being seen as rude by someone if that protects your physical and mental health. If saying a polite but firm no to someone is rude, then think about what you are opening yourself up to. You simply can't "yes" to everyone that wants something from you. This would be exhausting and dangerous.

Practice your "no" like you would practice an important speech in front of the mirror. Look for the way your eyes and body rest. Pay attention to your body language and note down how saying it makes you feel. Are you feeling stressed and anxious or maybe a sense of relief and empowerment? The first few times you will have to use it, especially if you never say it, might feel awkward and jumpy. But like everything else, practice makes perfect. When you practice saying no, you can create little dialogues where someone would try to turn your no into a yes. So after you have already said no to something, how could they try to change your mind? Manipulators are some of the most stubborn people there are so it is not just the first no you have to practice but the five that will have to follow afterwards. The more you learn to say no, the better you can protect yourself from manipulative people.

3. Stop Playing Their Game

The best thing you can do when a manipulator is baiting you is to ignore them. But that is easier said that done of course. When dealing with a distant friend, or work colleague this might even be an option. You simply can walk away and stop paying attention to what they say or do. Even with your relationships though, you have every right to cut off communication and resolve things fast.

Manipulators hate it when they are being ignored. While you are trying to stay calm and collected to avoid conflict it seems like they are fueling the fire and saying things that will make you emotional and cause you to lash out. This is done on purpose.

An emotional outburst is the moment you are showing your weaknesses. You are showing what words get to you or hurt you, and what triggers you. This is gold information they will use next time and also gives them the satisfaction of pushing your buttons and knowing how to make you do things.

It is vital you stay calm and collected and show no irritation or annoyance with their words even if they are making you very upset. It is best to step away from their presence in a calm and nonchalant way, collect your thoughts and not give in to their baiting.

4. Possess a Great Sense of Purpose

A person who is driven by destiny is harder to control and fool. One reason for the high success rates of manipulators is that a lot of us lack a sense of purpose. Even when we do, it tends to be insufficient. Someone who has no destiny, or sense of direction can do anything and believe things easily since they have no specific goals and plans. If a manipulator ever comes into contact with such a person, swaying them is a simple task. When you lack a sense of purpose, you have no idea why you live or where your life is heading. To the manipulator, you are an empty vessel that they can fill with their malice.

So, to keep manipulation and control away, you need to have a clear path in life, which leads to a specific goal. With this simple plan, you become harder to distract. One way to tell if you lack a sense of purpose is to evaluate how much time you use on reality TV, celebrity gossip, parties, uncontrolled hangouts, and other not-so-beneficial activities. If you use a lot of time on such, then it means your life has a void which you try to fill with these activities. Therefore, you are likely to embrace a manipulator when they approach you with "plans," not knowing they will be using you while destroying your life. When you are sure about your destination and the road to get there, nobody can misguide or distract you.

5. Always Stay True to Your Values and Opinions

The path to manipulation is not straight cut. Like we have discussed all throughout the book, there is a steady path from friend or lover to manipulator and it requires you seize over some control steadily so the manipulator can keep gaining ground. One of the best ways to protect yourself from being manipulated is to stay true to your values and opinions. That doesn't mean having disrespectful arguments or screaming matches. Quite the opposite in fact.

When a manipulator wants to see how malleable you are to outside forces, or his or her forces, they might try to bend you into agreeing with their position on certain arguments. These could be as simple as where you should eat, which pair of glasses suits you the most and go all the way up to your political beliefs. Of course not everyone that is trying to change your opinion will be doing so because they are trying to gain something. Sometimes they might really just don't like the glasses or dress or shoes you are wearing. But if you notice a partner or close friend is repeatedly trying to charm you into changing your actions and you are always going along with it, try to see what happens when you stick with what you want for a change. Thank them for their opinion but don't back down from saying you like a certain movie, or song. If the reaction is unjustified and they keep pushing for you to see things from their perspective then manipulation bells should start ringing.

6. Evaluate Apologies Logically Not Emotionally

Apologizing is part of everyday life. We all have had to do it sometimes and the most sincere and honest apologies are those that come from people that truly mean it. When you do it correctly, you take responsibility for what you did and don't include a whole bunch of "buts" and "ifs" or try to minimize the reasons for why someone is hurting. We apologize when we have hurt someone's feelings, because those feelings are valid and because if we care for them we will not want to put them in situations where they are hurting. So it doesn't matter that if it were us, we wouldn't have been offended by what they said. All that matters is that it bothered the other person, so you have to apologize.

With that in mind, there is such a thing as a good and a bad apology. Manipulators are not capable of accepting wrongdoing or recognize they hurt someone's feelings. They are master gas lighters and will eventually need to turn things around so they can blame you. So if you notice that their apology does not fit with some of the things described below, then you know they are not genuine.

First of all, a good apology is one that includes the words "I am sorry". You need to actually say that instead of tiptoeing around it. Phrases like "I am sorry for how you feel", or "I am sorry I hurt you" are taking the focus away from the person that should be doing the apologizing and on to you. Manipulators are great at trying to apologize for others' feelings even though they are the ones that caused it in the first place. Another key aspect is that a proper apology doesn't focus on intent. This is not a moment for the other person to explain the reasons that led them there but to say sorry.

Emotional manipulators are really good at turning the tables so much that you end up being the one apologizing to them or at least feeling sorry for them. So, they start off saying they are "Sorry I forgot your present" but then go on a pity party story about how they have been so stressed working overtime, and they are trying to be strong and not show it and they didn't want to trouble you with it. The pain is so great but at least they thought you understood them and wouldn't cause an issue about a silly present. How selfish could you be to only focus on what you want.

Because apologies are tense moments with lots of emotions we need to remember both the words people use and how they made us feel. If you get a weird feeling that they were not sincere, or if they refused to use the words and instead tried to blame you, then you need reevaluate your relationship to that person.

7. Delay Big Decisions aka "Sleep on It"

Some types of manipulation are insidious and not necessarily by how big they are but the opposite. Small moments of manipulation, however, can wear down your natural defenses and make you feel vulnerable and like you are lacking self-control and have no say. In your everyday life, these can be an agent trying to make you sign the lease on a house you are not sure of, or a friend asking you for a small loan, or your partner pushing you into a relationship decision before you had time to consider it.

The best thing to do in these situations is to ask for extra time and make it very clear you will not be giving an answer until you have had time to thoroughly think about it. Sometimes, there is no time to consider all the points or sides of an argument and need to step away from it and think clearly. Manipulators will not take that easily and will demand an answer straight away. They might present very convincing arguments that sound as though you would be a fool not to agree. They might even appeal to your emotional side and try to strong arm you into making decisions. This is especially true in sales, and smart salesmen will be very fast at breaking down your defenses. But if you do give in, then you are slowly telling your brain that your opinion and your thoughts are easily swayed. You might start to doubt your opinions and rely instead on what other people think is best.

Be polite but firm and ask for extra time to think about it. This will allow you to really understand what you want to do before presenting your answer.

8. Get a Second "Objective" Opinion

As mentioned above, being secure in your opinion is very important and builds trust and confidence in yourself. However, there are sometimes when a second opinion could also be very useful. Especially, if you are dealing with an issue where you know something is wrong but have been slowly made to see it otherwise. This is when the objective opinion of a friend or someone close to you but not directly involved could come in handy.

It is not just their opinion that can be useful in these situations but the process of explaining the situation to them in order to ask for their opinion. For example, you might have doubts about your partners behavior but every time you try to confront them about it they are being defensive and making you feel as though you are the problem. You sit down and try to talk to a friend about it and as you start talking you listen to your words for the first time and can see what the problem is before they have even said anything. Or maybe as you go along unpacking the situation, your friend makes a comment that makes you click.

When we are too close to a certain problem it can be hard to see with fresh eyes, so explaining the situation to someone is a useful tip when you are struggling with manipulative behavior. Remember also, getting a second opinion or talking to a friend about issues you are having is important, especially if you have always been the kind of person to share. When we keep everything bottled inside it is easier for someone to come and manipulate us.

9. Don't Rely on Your Memory

Our memory is easy to fail us. We think we said or did one thing then we did another. Or maybe the other person said something to us, and we heard only what we wanted to hear. One of the things manipulators do best is bending the truth and messing with our memories. This is bad for a number of reasons. We are slowly not able to trust what we think is true, and we are more likely to believe the things that they will then introduce to us.

In situations where you feel you are starting to get played and there is information that you don't remember or denial when you confront them with something they said, you can keep a small journal of what was said and done. When you are dealing with a manipulator, whether or not the truth is recorded will not make a difference to them of course. They will still try to find a way to wiggle their way out of it and present some other version of the truth. The record is more for you, so you don't start to doubt your memories of what happened.

While it is great if you want to keep a journal with what happened and what was said with people in your life, keep in mind that everyday people will not be so happy if they feel you are recording them or writing down everything in order to attack them with it later. Normal people will find ways to apologize and make peace in arguments without you bringing out the "fact sheet" that you have carefully recorded. And manipulators will not change their ways even if you do.

So if you do choose to keep a record of important conversations, know that it is mostly for yourself and your own mental health and not to prove it to someone else.

CONCLUSION

Thank you for reading all this book!

Finally, as you finish up, remember always to keep your use of persuasion ethical. Always ask yourself if you need to tap into the mind of someone else. Ask yourself if the other person is the primary beneficiary if you do happen to tap into their mind. Ask yourself if they will be happy to have the results of you tapping into their mind. If you can answer that they will benefit significantly and appreciate it, it may be a good time to use your arts.

You have already taken a step towards your improvement.

Best wishes!

CPSIA information can be obtained
at www.ICGtesting.com
Printed in the USA
BVHW090113040521
606332BV00005B/822